Growing in My Garden

Herbert Brunkhorst
&
Bonnie Brunkhorst

DOMINIE PRESS
Pearson Learning Group

Publisher: Christine Yuen
Series Editors: Adria F. Klein & Alan Trussell-Cullen
Editors: Bob Rowland & Paige Sanderson
Photographers: Nancy Lee & Y. Raymond
Designers: Gary Hamada, Lois Stanfield, & Vincent Mao

Photo Credits: Graham Meadows (Page 12-caterpillar;
Page 14-butterfly; Page 16-spider web).

Published by:

ᴪ Dominie Press, Inc.

1949 Kellogg Avenue
Carlsbad, California 92008 USA

www.dominie.com

ISBN 0-7685-0566-6

Printed in Singapore by PH Productions Pte Ltd

6 PH 07

Table of Contents

Cosmos
Bright Lights Mixed Colors

NET WT
500 mg

$1.19

To grow well, plants
need sun, water, and
good soil.

Dad helped us start
our own garden.

"Is the soil warm and ready
for growing our flower seeds
and our strawberry plant?"
asked Celina.

"Yes, the soil is ready,"
said Dad.
"We will put the flower seeds
half an inch deep
and cover them with soil."

"What about the strawberry plant?" asked Celina.

"We will plant the strawberry plant in a big hole," said Dad. "We have to cover all of its roots with soil."

"The flower seeds and
the strawberry plant will need
water to grow," said Celina.

"They will need sunshine, too,"
said John.

"Look how our plants have grown!" said Celina. "We have a flower on our flower plant."

"We have some flowers and a lot of strawberries on our strawberry plant!" said John.

"Look at this green bug,"
said Celina.

"The bug is eating
our strawberry plant!"
shouted John.
"It is eating the leaves."

"Look, there is a butterfly on the flower," said Celina. "Do you think it will eat the flower?"

"Wow!" shouted John.
"The bug just fell into a
spider web. The spider
is going to eat the bug."

"Let's pick this flower before a bug eats it," said Celina.

"Let's pick the strawberries before a bug eats them, too," said John.

Picture Glossary

butterfly:

soil:

flower:

strawberry:

Index